Theory Paper Grade 5   2016   A
Model Answers

music.

1 (a) (i) 1 diminished 5th   (2)
                2 major 6th   (2)
                3 perfect 11th / compound perfect 4th   (2)

(ii)   (3)

(b) Chord **A**   IV root / IVa   (2)
     Chord **B**   II 3rd / IIb   (2)
     Chord **C**   I 5th / Ic   (2)

2   (10)

3 (a) (i) peaceful / calm / serene / tranquil   (2)
                smoothly / slurred   (2)
          (ii) D   (2)

(iii)   (4)

(b) (i)   (2)

or

(ii) compound   (1)
      triple   (1)

(iii) **A** subdominant   **B** supertonic   (4)

3

(iv) (2)

(c) (i) false (2)
true (2)
(ii) baritone (2)
(iii) | | Instrument | cello / double bass / bass / harp | Family | strings | (4) |
| or | Instrument | bassoon | Family | woodwind | |
| or | Instrument | horn / trombone / tuba / bass tuba | Family | brass | |

4 (10)

(a)

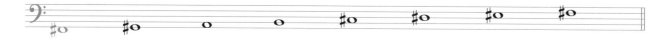

(b)

5 (10)

6 *There are many ways of completing this question. Either of the specimen completions below would receive full marks.* (15)

EITHER

(a) trumpet

Alla marcia

OR

(b)

Andante cantabile

I have made____ for you a song,____ And it may____ be right or wrong.

7   EITHER   (10)

(a)   Chord A   II / A minor   Chord D   IV / C major
       Chord B   V / D major   Chord E   I / G major
       Chord C   I / G major

OR

(b)

Theory Paper Grade 5   2016   B
Model Answers

1

    (a)   (6)

    (b)   (i)   Chord **A**   I 3rd / Ib   (2)
               Chord **B**   IV root / IVa   (2)
       (ii) turn / upper turn   (2)

       (iii)   (3)

2 1   diminished 5th   (10)

      2   minor 6th

      3   diminished 7th

      4   augmented 2nd

      5   major 10th / compound major 3rd

3   (10)

4   (a)   (i)   *All possible answers are shown on the extract reproduced below. For full marks candidates need to identify only one example of each answer.*

                  B   Bar 1   (2)

                  C   Bar 8   (2)

                  D   Bar 4 / 5   (2)

          (ii)   (4)

   (b)   (i)   comfortably / conveniently   (2)

                          always / ever   (2)

                          emphatic / accented / marked / stressed   (2)

                          forced / forcing / accented   (2)

          (ii)   G major   (2)

   (c)   (i)   true   (2)

                          false   (2)

	(ii)		Instrument	cello / double bass / bass / harp	Family	strings	(4)
		or	Instrument	bassoon / double bassoon	Family	woodwind	
		or	Instrument	horn / trombone / tuba / bass tuba	Family	brass	
	(iii)					<u>marimba</u>	(2)

5 (10)

(a)

(b)

6 *There are many ways of completing this question. Either of the specimen completions below would receive full marks.* (15)

EITHER

(a) flute

OR

(b)

And on the bay the__ moon - light lay, And the sha - dow of__ the moon.

7 EITHER (10)

(a) Chord A   II / E minor   Chord D   IV / G major
Chord B   IV / G major   Chord E   I / D major
Chord C   V / A major

OR

7

(b)

Theory Paper Grade 5   2016   C
Model Answers

1

    (a)   Bar 1: **⁶₈**   Bar 2: **⁷₈**   Bar 3: **⁵₈**   (6)

    (b)   (i)   Chord **A**   IV 3rd / IVb   (2)
                   Chord **B**   II 3rd / IIb   (2)

        (ii)   (2)

Ic – V
or ⁶₄ – ⁵₃

        (iii)   (3)

2 1   augmented 2nd   (10)
    2   augmented 4th
    3   diminished 12th / compound diminished 5th
    4   minor 7th
    5   major 6th

3

(10)

4 (a) (i) with movement / with motion / moving (2)

agitated / restless (2)

pause on the note / hold on to the note (2)

(ii) two / two quavers / two eighth notes / one crotchet / (2)
one quarter note / one beat

(iii) turn / upper turn (2)

(b) (i) (4)

(ii) X mediant (2)

Y leading note (2)

(iii) F♯ (2)

(c) (i) (2)

(ii) brass (2)

tuba / bass tuba (2)

(iii) Definite pitch   timpani / kettledrums / xylophone / marimba / glockenspiel / (2)
vibraphone / celesta / tubular bells

Indefinite pitch   side drum / snare drum / bass drum / cymbals / triangle / (2)
tambourine / castanets / tam-tam

5 (10)

(a)

(b)

6 *There are many ways of completing this question. Either of the specimen completions below would receive full marks.* (15)

EITHER

(a)   cello

OR

(b)

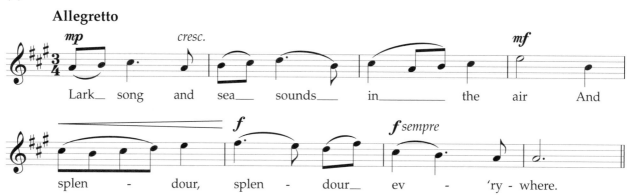

7   EITHER (10)

(a)   Chord A   IV / F major   Chord C   II / D minor
       Chord B   I / C major   Chord D   V / G major
                                        Chord E   I / C major

OR

(b)

Theory Paper Grade 5   2016   S
Model Answers

1 (a) (i) Chord **A**   IV 3rd / IVb   (2)
                Chord **B**   I 5th / Ic   (2)
                Chord **C**   V root / Va   (2)
           (ii) B♭ major   (2)

   (b) (i)   (3)

        (ii)   (2)

             or

             or

        (iii) demisemiquaver / 32nd note   (2)

2   (10)

3 (a) (i) play the notes in quick succession starting from the bottom note / arpeggiation /   (2)
                spread the chord from the bottom to the top
                agitated / restless   (2)
                gradually getting faster   (2)

        (ii)   (4)

   (b) (i)   1   minor 7th   (2)
              2   major 10th / compound major 3rd   (2)
              3   augmented 4th   (2)

(4)

(c) (i) C   (2)

    (ii) **A** mediant   (2)

        B submediant   (2)

    (iii)   *Family*   woodwind   *Instrument*   flute / piccolo   (4)

      or   *Family*   brass   *Instrument*   trumpet

      or   *Family*   percussion   *Instrument*   glockenspiel / xylophone / celesta

4   (10)

(a)

(b)

5   (10)

6   *There are many ways of completing this question. Either of the specimen completions below would receive full marks.*   (15)

EITHER

(a)   bassoon

OR

12

(b)

And hand_ in hand, on the edge of the sand, They danced_____ by the light of the moon.

7 EITHER   (10)

(a)   Chord A   IV / C major   Chord C   II / A minor
       Chord B   I / G major   Chord D   I / G major
                                      Chord E   V / D major

OR

(b)

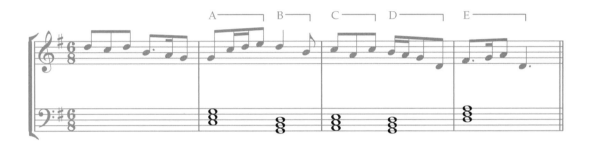